A YEAR IN THE LIFE
CHIMPANZEE

John Stidworthy/Gill Tomblin

Silver Burdett Press

Conceived and produced by
Lionheart Books
10 Chelmsford Square
London NW10 3AR

Editor Lionel Bender,
assisted by Madeleine Samuel
Editor, U.S. edition Joanne Fink
Designer Ben White

From an original idea by
Lionel Bender and Dr. J. F. Oates,
Primatologist, Hunter College,
New York

Copyright © Lionheart Books 1987

© 1988–this adaptation
Silver Burdett Press

Published in the United States
in 1988 by Silver Burdett Press,
Morristown, New Jersey

**Library of Congress Cataloging-in-
Publication Data**

Stidworthy, John, 1943-
    Chimpanzee.

    (A Year in the life)
    Includes index.
    Summary: Presents a year in the
life of a young chimpanzee who lives
with his mother in a rain forest in East
Africa.
    1. Chimpanzees--Juvenile
literature. [1. Chimpanzees]
I. Tomblin, Gill, ill. II. Title
III. Series: Stidworthy, John, 1943-
Year in the life.
QL737.P96S75   1988   599.88'44
87-16631
ISBN 0-382-09519-7
ISBN 0-382-09521-9 (pbk.)

A YEAR IN THE LIFE: CHIMPANZEE
Written by John Stidworthy
Illustrated by Gill Tomblin

ABOUT THIS BOOK

Our book tells the story of the life of one particular chimpanzee over a single year. We have written and illustrated our story as if we had watched the chimp's behavior through the year, noticing how its activities changed at different periods. By looking closely at one chimp, we give you a good understanding of how an individual animal reacts to others and to the conditions it experiences in the wild.

We have called our chimpanzee Pan. On pages 4 and 5 we show you where Pan lives and tell you a little about Pan's habits and lifestyle. Our main story, on pages 6 to 29, follows a year in Pan's life, and is divided up into six sections between one and three months long. Each section begins with a large illustration showing the environment and one aspect of Pan's behavior at that time. The following two pages in each section continue our main story and show some of Pan's other activities during the same period. On page 30 we discuss chimpanzee conservation.

INTRODUCTION

Apes, unlike monkeys, have no tails and their arms are longer than their legs. There are four types of ape. The small gibbons live in Southeast Asia. More closely related to us are the great apes: the chimpanzees, gorillas, and orangutans. Of these, the chimpanzees may be our closest living relations. The apes are well adapted for climbing trees. They can grasp with hands and feet and their long arms allow them to swing from branch to branch. Chimpanzees find much of their food in trees, but they are also good at moving on the ground. They can stand upright, but normally walk on all fours.

Chimpanzees are forest animals, although some go into open country. They usually live in groups, but they do not always stay in the same group for long. The most constant group is a mother and her baby and any growing young, who remain with her until they are about 10 years old.

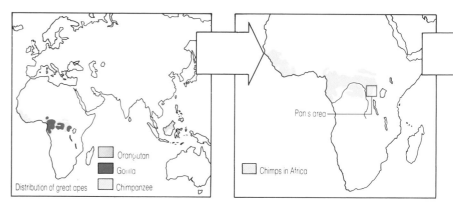

△ Chimpanzees, scientific name *Pan troglodytes*, are found in forests from Senegal east to Tanzania. Our chimp, Pan, lives in an area that is mostly low-lying forest, with some clearings.

△ Orangutans live in forests in Borneo and Sumatra, chimpanzees and gorillas in equatorial Africa. Their homes are disappearing as forests are cut down to make way for farmland.

4

Our chimpanzee Pan

A mother and her young may join with others to form a large group. Some groups consist of only males, others are mixed. The make-up of groups keeps changing as adult chimps join and leave. Together, all the chimpanzees in an area form a loose "tribe" which protects that area from strangers.

Our story is about a young chimpanzee, Pan. He lives with his mother in a rain forest in east Africa.

The seasons

In Pan's part of Africa there is no winter. But there are distinct seasons. From May to October it seldom rains; the ground and some plants dry in the hot sun. From October to April there is rain, and it is especially heavy from early December to February. Then the grass may grow over 6 feet high. At some times there is more food than at others, but the chimps can always find some edible fruits or leaves within their area.

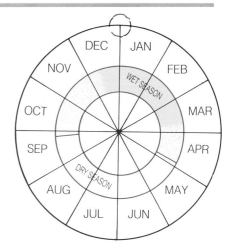

△ The calendar in Pan's range. A small calendar is used in the book to show the time span of each section.

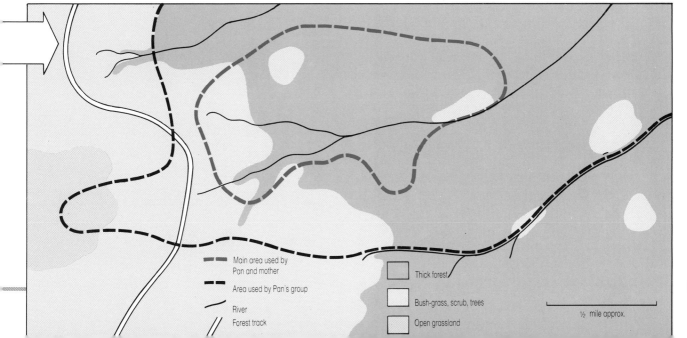

- - - Main area used by Pan and mother

- - - Area used by Pan's group

—— River

// Forest track

☐ Thick forest

☐ Bush-grass, scrub, trees

☐ Open grassland

½ mile approx.

5

IN THE FOREST

Pan rode on his mother's back as she walked along a thick branch nearly 60 feet above the ground. He was used to being carried this way, and felt safe even though the branch swayed. His mother walked on all fours. The soles of her feet and the knuckles of her hands rested on the branch.

Pan was a young male chimpanzee about four years old. He could move around by himself, but he still liked a lift from his mother if he could get one. It was the hottest and driest part of the year. Outside the forest the sun was beating down, but in the shade of the tallest trees the temperature was comfortable. Although the grass outside the forest was brown and shriveled, and even the forest floor was dry, the chimpanzees rarely went without food for long. Even now some of the forest trees came into fruit and the chimps wandered until they found something worth eating.

Some days Pan and his mother were alone as they moved through the forest. Other days they met more chimpanzees, sometimes just one or two, other times a big party. They did not follow any set route through the forest. Mostly they wandered as their fancy and hunger took them. When a favorite tree was in fruit they might visit it several days in a row, but they had no fixed "home" to which they returned. However, Pan's mother had been living in the same area ever since she was born 30 years before, and knew it well. As he grew, Pan too was learning much about the area.

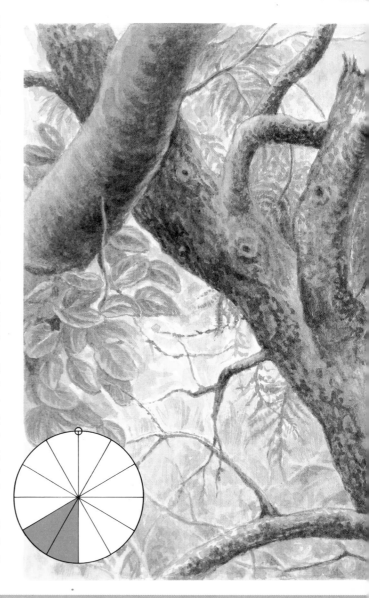

◁◁ Forward-facing eyes help chimpanzees judge distances when they are climbing. Their noses are small but scent is important to them. They make many sounds, and their ears can pick up calls of other chimps many miles away.

▷ When a chimp can sit close enough to plant food it may pull leaves, fruits, or nuts right off with its teeth and lips. Otherwise it will reach out for them with its hands. Youngsters often practise climbing as they forage and "play".

◁ Young chimpanzees have rounder faces than adults and their hair is often lighter colored. Adults have darker, craggier faces.

Aware and alert

Pan was curious about his surroundings and interested in new objects. If he saw other animals and they seemed strange, he took refuge behind his mother and peered at them. She was more confident but was always quick to notice the occasional danger. She was also more aware of food and the signs or sounds of chimps.

Like all chimps, Pan and his mother had excellent vision and a good sense of color. They could often tell from the ground whether fruits in the trees were ripe. Sometimes, though, they had to get close enough to sniff food before they could tell if it was just as they wanted. Some of the fruit they enjoyed would taste very bitter to humans.

As they went through the forest Pan and his mother at times moved through the trees, and occasionally along the ground. They were equally adept in either place.

▷ Chimpanzee babies start to eat solid food at about 4 months old, but breast milk is important to them up until about 3 years old. Their mother usually stops suckling them by 5 years old.

Food and foraging

One morning Pan and his mother found a tree full of figs that had just ripened and had not yet been plundered by other chimpanzees or even the birds and monkeys. Pleased with their find, they quickly climbed up and began cramming the fruit into their mouths. They fed until they were full.

Later, while his mother sat contented on the ground, Pan swung from some low branches by his arms. Then he jumped down to the ground, where he started exploring. Everything he found he put in his mouth. He rolled a hard fruit around his lips as a plaything, feeling its texture and shape.

▷ Chimps often swing by the arms to move through trees. Going up a trunk they may put their arms around the trunk and "walk" up with their legs.

No longer a baby

Pan was now getting a bit too heavy to ride on his mother's back, and she began to discourage him, either pulling him off with her hand or moving away if he tried to climb on. It was the same with suckling. Pan was old enough to feed without needing milk, but he still went to his mother to suckle if he got the chance. It was comforting to him, and his mother sometimes allowed it when she could feel he was tired. But often nowadays she would wave him away with an impatient shake of the arm.

While Pan had been tiny, his mother had kept apart from most of the chimpanzees in the area, although she and Pan sometimes spent several days at a time in the company of other mothers with babies. Now that Pan was larger she was less anxious. In fact, as the dry season drew to a close Pan's mother started to come into breeding condition again. She felt the need

10

for the companionship of other adults, especially the males. At first Pan was nervous of the big males, but most ignored him, and he soon began with playing with other youngsters.

After they had fed well in the morning, the chimpanzees rested and relaxed. Then they indulged in one of their favorite activities, grooming. Sometimes they groomed themselves, but often they would groom one another. It was a mark of friendliness and respect. The adolescents of the group mostly groomed the adults. The chimps huddled together, parting fur and picking off salty pieces of old skin and the odd insect. Often they found little to remove, but the sensation was pleasant.

Pan was too young to join with the adult groomers. He was groomed by his mother. He enjoyed her touch, but sometimes he got bored and tried to escape. She would pin him down if necessary until she was finished. Pan spent his time doing whatever he liked, but his mother made sure he was groomed regularly, and that he did not venture far from her side.

One morning, while Pan sat in a clearing close to a group of grooming males, clouds started to move swiftly across the sky. A few drops of rain fell, the first of a new rainy season.

Learning one's place in society

Most of the time the chimpanzees got along well together, but some, and particularly one of the big old males, always managed to get the best food and the best resting places. In fact, among both males and females there was a system of rank or status, with less dominant animals giving in to those above them. Pan learned that a young chimpanzee was expected to give way to his or her elders. But Pan's mother was one of the high-ranking females, and this

△ Adult male chimps may be much bigger and heavier than females. Young chimps often have a tuft of white hair on their behinds.

gave Pan a higher status than many of the other youngsters. When feeding, they would often leave Pan the choicest fruits.

Generally Pan did not worry about such things. He just treated adults warily and played with as many of the young chimps as he was allowed to. But as he grew up he would find that rank was very important in chimpanzee society.

◁ The swollen pink behind of a female chimp indicates she is ready to mate. This occurs every 5 weeks except when she is pregnant or suckling.

No mating this time

By now Pan's mother was in full breeding condition, with a swollen pink bottom, but she did not mate. Although several males took an interest in her, she did not encourage any of them. The time for mating passed, and the pink swelling went down again. But from this time on Pan and his mother joined with groups more often.

△ One chimp will signal to another that it is giving way and accepting the other as superior by turning its back and crouching low before him or her.

New experiences

In this way Pan came to learn what the adult chimpanzees in the neighborhood were like. Sometimes he was curious about food the old males were eating and tried to edge closer. Usually the eater hunched over the food, shutting Pan out, or grunted crossly to keep him away. But one day two adult males engrossed in chewing shreds from a shrub did not shoo him away. Pan came closer, rather nervously, but the big male let him come alongside. Then the

△ Adult male chimps can be tolerant of young ones and pat or touch them as a sign of friendship or to stop them from being frightened. Chimps are good at reading each other's moods by their gestures.

adult reached out and patted Pan gently. Pan had been accepted. He sat watching and the male took a few of the plant fibers from his mouth and gave some to Pan. Pan tried them. They tasted gingery and rather strange. He was not sure he liked the taste, but he sat chewing with the big chimps for a while.

A minor dispute

Happy with his meeting with the adult males, Pan returned to the group of mothers and their young. He now felt in a playful mood, and scampered about looking for playmates.

He tried to play with several youngsters, but picked one that was too young. Its mother got cross and nervous and chased him away. At this Pan's own mother charged at the other mother, who gave way, signaling that she accepted her as the dominant animal.

A NEW TYPE OF FOOD

Once the rains began it poured most days. The hard ground softened and plants spurted into growth. Outside the forest the dead brown grass gave way to new green shoots. Pan did not like rain, but he enjoyed some of the plant foods that grew when it was wet. Also at this time of year there was another food that was good. When the ground was dry termites in the forest stayed underground. Their nests showed above the forest floor as hard-baked mounds of mud. Now the rains had come, these insects were near the surface. The older chimpanzees recognized the signs of this, and began examining the nests they came across.

One afternoon Pan's mother started foraging at a termite mound. At first Pan went on playing, but then he became fascinated by what his mother was doing and leaned close, watching intently. She was poking a stick down a hole in the nest. It did not go in as she wanted and she picked another stem from a nearby shrub and carefully pulled off leaves. Then she poked the stem down the hole. When she pulled it out termites were clinging to the end. Quickly she bent and picked them off with her lips. She kept on dipping and eventually she allowed Pan to try this new delicacy. Another family joined them at the nest, and for an hour or more all the animals fed on the termites. Pan tried poking with a twig, but it was a long time before he scooped any out.

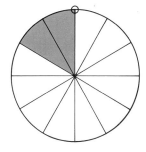

Mating takes place

Once again Pan's mother was coming into breeding condition. She met a small group of males and one of them moved off with Pan and his mother. He stayed with them for the next two weeks, and mated with Pan's mother many times. When he was ready to mate he attracted her attention by sitting upright and shaking branches with one hand. When she looked away he held out his arm toward her. She moved to the male and crouched in front of him on all fours. They mated briefly, the male still sitting on the ground. Usually Pan took little notice of them, but sometimes he came close, occasionally even getting in the way or peering into the male's or his mother's face out of curiosity and fascination.

The adults ignored Pan when they were mating, but at other times the male was easily irritated by the antics of the small chimpanzee. He was used to a quiet life with other adults. One day, as Pan crashed through the bushes next to him while he was eating, the male lost his temper.

△▷ A female chimp in breeding condition may be led away and kept by a single male chimp, who discourages others from approaching. But often she will join a group of several males, and will mate repeatedly with as many of them as are interested in her.

He flung out an arm toward Pan then leaped up with a bark, his hair on end, and chased after Pan. He caught up with him, grabbed Pan and bit him, then slowly stalked back to his food. After a few moments he was feeding quietly again.

◁ Threats in chimps range from a flick of the forearm, to an enraged display with screams, shaking of vegetation, and charges toward an opponent.

△ Chimps drink little as their food is juicy, but may drink water from streams or tree hollows. They may crumple up leaves to use as a sponge.

Feeding on a carcass

Pan was so stunned by the male's attack that for a moment he did not move. Then he whimpered and ran to his mother's side and clutched her. He had not been hurt much, but it had been a shock. In the future he was more careful with adults unless he was sure they were friendly.

Pan learned other lessons from the old male, who one day killed a monkey that came close. The male fed on its meat, and allowed Pan and his mother to share his catch. Pan had not eaten meat before, and he seldom did so again, yet it was to form a part of his diet.

Days later, the male left Pan and his mother, and once more they were alone.

TREE-LIVING

The heaviest rains of the year had arrived. Every day there was a downpour, and some days it rained for hours. There were enormous thunderstorms that rolled around the valleys, and lightning crackled over the hills. Water dripped from the trees almost continuously. When the sun came out steam rose from the ground and trees. The chimpanzees were excited by the storms, and Pan could hear groups hooting and calling from far away. But they did not enjoy getting soaking wet. It was less hot than a few months ago, but the dampness made it feel sticky.

Often the best times of Pan's day were in the evening when the day's rain had stopped and everything had dried a little. He fed in comfort for a while, gathering his supper before he and his mother found somewhere to sleep. Each night they climbed a suitable tree and made a hammock to rest on. This was constructed, usually by Pan's mother, by bending in flexible branches to the point where she was sitting, weaving them into a springy platform that could take her weight. Pan used to sleep in the same nest, but now he preferred his own little nest close to hers. Once made, the chimpanzees stayed in their nests all twelve hours of the night. They were not asleep all this time, but had no wish to leave the relative safety of the nest when it was too dark to see clearly. If the morning was dry they were active soon after dawn, but in the wet weather they seemed reluctant to start the day.

◁ When it rains hard chimpanzees hunch themselves up and sit still. Sometimes they build a nest and sit in it. But they do not seem to think of taking shelter, and so get soaking wet.

▽ Chimpanzees may build nests as high as 145 feet up a big tree, but commonly they construct their beds about 30 feet up. Here they lie on their sides and sleep.

The daily routine

When it rained hard, the chimpanzees stopped feeding or moving around and just sat waiting for it to stop. When it ceased they shook themselves and carried on with normal life. Generally they were active early in the morning and by mid-day were resting again. They were back in action in the afternoon and just before dark, but were not so hungry as in the morning. The things they ate were bulky, but often not very nutritious. Also, they digested the food quite quickly, so they needed to eat a lot of it.

During the day Pan and his mother rested whenever they felt the need, but just occasionally, up a tree, Pan's mother would weave a quick version of the night-time nest.

One day Pan and his mother entered a clearing in the forest and met a dozen other chimpanzees they knew already there. They were greeted by some of the nearest, and when the group moved on the two chimps stayed with them. Pan enjoyed playing with two young chimpanzees in the group.

The next day, the group Pan was in met with another group almost as large, by the bank of one of the forest streams. The excitement was terrific. The animals all knew one another, but this did not stop the two groups from rushing about and showing off to each other.

△▷ During meetings between groups, males especially stamp and charge to impress "opponents." Youngsters watch and later copy their elders.

△ Friendly chimps may greet with hugs. Often sisters or brothers remain friends throughout their lives, although they spend much of their time apart.

One big, happy, noisy family

Most excited of all the chimps were the adult males. They drew themselves to their full height, hair bristling, and shook branches. Some screamed and charged at the newcomers, giving them a hearty pat on the back as they swerved off into the forest. Others dragged branches with them as they charged, making a loud scrapping and rustling noise. The noisiest of all found some tall trees with flat buttress roots and banged on these with their hands and feet. The roots acted like huge drums and the sound boomed out into the forest and could be heard several miles away.

In spite of all the bustle and pandemonium none of the chimpanzees came to any harm and twenty minutes later the whole group started to feed quietly again. In the meantime Pan's mother had reunited with one of her sisters. It was several months since they had seen each other and they touched lips and hugged one another. Then they sat side by side, first as the group fed and then, as it rested, grooming one another. Pan peered at his aunt and she looked at him and tried to groom him. Although he did not know her very well, he felt comfortable with this friendly chimpanzee.

Most of the foods the chimpanzees ate could just be picked and eaten, although some needed a lot of chewing. A few kinds they chewed to get out the juice and goodness, then spat out the ball of stringy fibers that were left. But there were some foods that were difficult to reach, and for these Pan relied on the skill of his mother. She could poke out the fruits of the oil palm from among all its spines and break off this tree's spiny fronds and strip away the hard outer covering to get at the pith beneath. Usually when she obtained food of this sort Pan's mother allowed him a share, but just occasionally she kept a special treat for herself. If she did not give him what he wanted, Pan threw a tantrum, flinging himself on the ground, screaming and waving his arms and legs. This made little difference, and his mother ignored him until he calmed down.

One or two of the fruits the chimps liked had very hard shells, which had to be cracked before getting at the pulp inside. They often used their canine teeth to start a crack, but one day they found fruits much too hard even for their strong teeth. Pan gave up trying to open them, and instead used them as playthings. But his mother knew how to tackle them. She banged them hard against a tree trunk, and battered them against a large stone on the ground until they opened. Then they moved on to another tree with berries that were easy to gather. They spent about half of each day, sometimes longer, gathering and eating food.

△▷ Noisy displays by one group directed at another seem designed to warn strangers off. Although they may make charges, chimp groups space themselves out without actual fighting.

Venture into an unknown area

One morning Pan found himself traveling with a small group that had in it three adult male chimpanzees, two young males about nine years old, and four females including his mother. They were right on the edge of the area Pan knew. They ventured out of the forest and climbed up the ridge of a hill. In the valley the grass was so tall after all the rain that it towered over the chimpanzees but now, as they went higher, the vegetation thinned out. They climbed where Pan had never been before. Even the big males were moving cautiously. It was the limit of "their" part of countryside. They came to the top of the ridge and sat peering out over the next valley beyond. Now, in the latter part of the rainy season, the sky was often cloudless, and the chimps could see far into the distance. On the far side of the valley was another expanse of forest similar to Pan's home.

Suddenly they heard chimpanzees hooting in the valley below. The watchers shifted around uneasily. Then at the bottom of the slope several black shapes emerged, crashing through the bushes and hooting. The males of Pan's troop started hooting and displaying in response. They crashed around, and threw sticks and rocks down the slope, but did not go down.

◁ A mother's touch quickly calms a nervous youngster. Care by a mother is important to a young chimp, which may not survive if its mother dies.

▽ Chimpanzees can solve some problems. A mother, realizing her young is too small to cross a gap, will bend branches to make a bridge.

Motherly love and protection

Pan was so frightened by the sudden din that he ran to his mother for comfort. She held out her hand and allowed him to cling to her, but he still went on watching as the males displayed. The young males imitated their elders but stayed well behind them. Then the display stopped as abruptly as it had begun, and the group turned and moved back down the hill. The chimps in the next valley disappeared into their own forest.

Both groups had claimed their right to a particular area and now went back to the job of finding food within it. They spent more time toward the middle of their area than near the edges, but every so often the males would patrol their borders, watching and listening for strangers.

Although Pan was interested in the displays he would not be taking part in them for a few years yet. But he had grown up a little. He had stopped suckling and he rarely tried to ride on his mother's back, but he still needed her help and care. Sometimes she seemed to guess if he was having difficulty doing something and would come and help or show him how it could be done.

INDEPENDENCE

The wet season was coming to a close. It rained often but not hard, then stopped completely. Pan hardly noticed the gradual change of season, but he felt the winds that sprang up early each morning. Then the weather calmed again and Pan enjoyed long hot sunny days. His mother allowed him to leave her side for longer now, and he made the most of this freedom. The two of them spent more time with other chimpanzees, often alongside mothers with young Pan's age or a little older. These were usually willing to wrestle or chase, and even if they were sitting quietly Pan could persuade them to join in by bouncing up and attracting their attention.

Sometimes there were older, nearly full-grown chimps around too, but Pan did not always get along so well with them. They tended to find the small chimpanzees too lively. Occasionally he got his ears boxed for butting in when he was not wanted. There were other times, though, when Pan's antics managed to involve the small chimps and the adolescents, and even an adult or two would join in.

In the group Pan was able to test the limits of what was allowed in chimpanzee society, and to discover more about the character of other chimps. This was important because he would be living in the group for many years. Pan was happy. There was plenty of company, lots to do and watch, and if anything went wrong there was always a mother to run back to. But soon Pan's mother would have someone else to look after. She had become pregnant from mating in November, and at the end of June the baby would be born.

27

△ Young chimps sometimes play with young baboons, but relations between adults are less friendly. They may fight, especially if both want the same food.

△ Chimpanzees avoid dangerous animals and ignore most others, although they take an interest in monkeys.

△ A forest tree may attract chimps from a wide area when it comes into fruit. The animals have a good memory and return to it the following year.

A variety of life

As well as playing with chimpanzees, Pan played games with other creatures. He tried poking with his fingers at the beetles and millipedes he saw in the forest, but they either stopped still or scuttled for cover. The long grey thing he saw sticking out from under a bush turned out to be a snake, and when it hissed he fled screaming to his mother. The colobus monkeys and squirrels in the trees were not much fun either. They stayed clear of him.

One day, though, the chimps were feeding alongside some baboons, and Pan played with one of the young ones. Both animals were a bit wary, but for a while they played. First one, then the other, made a little jump which the other dodged. The game ended when one of the big baboons saw what was happening and came rushing over, showing its teeth and barking at Pan, who hurriedly scrambled away out of reach.

Pan saw the baboons often over the next few days. One of the huge old fig trees in the forest had come into fruit. Nearly 30 chimps gathered there, and monkeys, including the baboon troop, also turned up to gorge on the fruit. Birds such as hornbills also came to feed on the figs, and for three days there was plenty for all the animals.

A sister for Pan

Gradually the party broke up and the chimps drifted away from the big tree. Not all went off in the same group they arrived in. Pan's mother was nearly due to have her baby and she felt the need for quiet. She wandered away, deeper into the forest, followed just by Pan.

One morning when Pan left his nest and moved to his mother he found she was clutching a tiny newborn baby and cleaning it carefully. She let him look, but pushed him away when he tried to touch. The new baby was a female. She started sucking motions with her lips, and fastened onto one teat when her mother held her to her breast. She was a strong baby, and after a few days she started to watch what was going on around her and Pan was allowed to touch her. Pan's mother was still affectionate to him but the baby got most of her love and care.

▷ Pregnancy lasts about 230 days in the chimpanzee. The baby is carried on the mother's front for the first few months, afterwards on her back. A chimp may live 40 years or more.

CONSERVATION

At one time chimpanzees probably lived throughout the forests of equatorial Africa. They are still widespread, but there are fewer than there used to be, and the population is in scattered pockets. In some places chimpanzees are thought to be good eating, and are hunted for meat. In the past many were also taken away for zoos and for use in laboratories. Zoos now breed chimpanzees, and should be able to help keep up the world population and not take more from the wild. Because chimps are so like us they are useful in research into human diseases. Unfortunately their similarity also means they can catch some of our diseases when wild populations come close to humans.

Perhaps the biggest threat to chimpanzees, as with many animals, is the disappearance of their living space. A group of chimps may require 10sq mi of forest in which to live, each animal wandering 3 miles a day. But as the number of people increases, forests are cut down for farmland, and there is less room for animals. Even when forests are cut down and replanted for timber the new trees are often types that are of no value to chimps.

But there is some hope. Wild chimpanzees have been studied more in the last 25 years than ever before, and we are more aware of their needs. Some areas have been set aside for them to live unmolested. Laws on conservation and on trade in endangered animals have cut out some hunting and poaching.

For further details
Useful information about chimp conservation can be obtained from the World Wildlife Fund, 1661 Connecticut Ave NW Washington, DC 20009.

▷ For chimps to survive in the wild, their forest home and fruit trees must be protected